The Essential Guide to

WEIGHT TRAINING

for Women

Robert Duffy Series Editor

Published in Great Britain in 2018 by
need2know
Remus House
Coltsfoot Drive
Peterborough
PE2 9BF
Telephone 01733 898103
www.need2knowbooks.co.uk

Contents

Plyometrics

Chapter 3: Weight Training for Fat Loss **35**

Chapter 4: Weight Training for Physique **45**

Chapter 5: Weight Training for Sport **55**

Chapter 6: Getting More from Your Weight Training **63**

Chapter 7: Injury Recovery and Prevention **75**

Help List **84**

Introduction

More and more people are coming to appreciate the importance of staying fit and active, and yet weight training is still an often overlooked form of exercise. The impression many have, when they think of weight training, is of bulky bodybuilders throwing around massive weights in dark, dirty gyms.

This impression is an unfair one. Weight training is important for people from all walks of life; men and women, young and old. Everyone can benefit from lifting heavy weights.

This book will help you to get started with weight training. It will begin by clarifying some common misconceptions, before moving on to explain how to perform the most popular weight training exercises in a safe and effective manner.

There are several different exercises covered in the book. Some of the exercises will require a barbell and a bench, while others can be done with just a small set of dumbbells. Whether you're planning on working out at the gym, or in your own home, there are exercises that will help you in this book. Some chapters in this book are devoted to weight training for a specific sport, while others cover weight training to improve your physique or lose weight.

This book is designed as a guide to help you get started with weight training. As you gain more experience you may find that you want to explore the activity in greater depth. To this end, you will find references to weight training organisations, including powerlifting and bodybuilding groups, as well as communities for people who enjoy lifting weights, at the end of this book.

'The impression many have of weight training is of bulky bodybuilders throwing around massive weights in dark, dirty gyms.'

Note

You may notice that "Calorie" is written with an upper case 'C' throughout this book. This is because we are talking about dietary Calories. There's another type of calorie (note the lower case 'c'), which is a unit of measurement that physicists use.

In physics, a calorie is also referred to as a gram calorie, or a thermodynamic calorie, which is based on the amount of energy required to raise the temperature of a gram of water by one degree Celsius. The dietary Calorie can also be referred to as a kilogram calorie - the amount of energy required to raise the temperature of a kilogram of water by one degree Celsius.

While it's rare to see references to thermodynamic calories outside of scientific publications, it's still worth remembering that such a unit of measurement exists. Writing "Calorie" with an upper case 'C' removes all doubt as to which unit is being used.

Disclaimer

When performed correctly, weight training is a safe and enjoyable sport, but with any physical activity there is always the risk of injury. You should always consult your doctor before beginning a new exercise routine, or making any major changes to your diet.

If you choose to train with barbells, then make sure that you have a friend with you to assist should you find yourself unable to complete a repetition of an exercise.

The author of this book does not claim any medical qualifications. If you have any doubts or concerns, or you experience discomfort during physical activity, cease activity immediately and consult your doctor.

1

Why Weight Training?

W eight training is one of the most overlooked forms of exercise. Many people, when they think of weight training, think of dark gyms full of sweaty, muscle bound men who scream and grunt as they lift, and would laugh at the average newcomer.

This image is unfair, and if you're avoiding lifting weights because of it, you're really missing out! Weight training is a great form of exercise for almost anyone – male or female. It makes you fitter and stronger, encourages your body to burn more Calories, and can increase your bone density, which is important for protecting you from osteoporosis as you get older.

Weight training is easy to get started with too. If you're one of the 4.5 million people in the UK that has a gym membership, you can train at your gym. If you don't have a gym membership, then you can get started at home with just a small amount of equipment.

This book is divided up into seven chapters. First you will learn a little about weight training and how it can benefit you, then you will learn some simple exercises for each of the major muscle groups. Chapters 3 through 5 will each look at a common fitness goal, and explain how you can use weight training as part of a fitness regime to achieve that goal.

The final few chapters will talk about more advanced workouts, preventing injuries and coping with them if they do happen, and how to get more information if you want to pursue one of the different forms of weight training as a hobby.

How can weightlifting help me achieve my fitness goals?

'If you're one of the 4.5 million people in the UK that has a gym membership, you can train at your gym.'

When you think of weight training, you probably think of getting really big and bulky. While this is something you could do if you wanted, it actually takes a lot of work – regular, specific exercises with heavy weights, and a very specific diet. Most people who lift weights don't look like the bodybuilders you see on the stage at the Mr Olympia contest, but they do enjoy the health benefits that weight training offers.

Weight training can help you to:

- Lose weight.
- Get stronger.
- Improve your performance in other sports.
- Improve your overall health and energy levels.
- Look better in that swimsuit or wedding dress.

Weight loss through weight training

If you have tried in the past to lose weight, and either been unsuccessful, or had trouble keeping the weight off long term, then weight training could help you.

Many people that I have spoken to have slaved away in the gym using the treadmill, exercise bike, or other cardio machines, and found that they were successful in losing weight by cutting down Calories and exercising regularly. However, they quickly lost interest because the long, demanding cardio workouts weren't viable long term.

Cardiovascular exercise is important for your overall health, but instead of tiring yourself out on the treadmill every day, why not reduce the number of cardio sessions you do and try lifting weights? Weight training increases your muscle mass, which means that your Base Metabolic Rate (BMR) increases. That means you burn more Calories, even while you're sat at the desk in your office.

Weight training for strength and sports

If you're a sportsperson, or someone who has a physically demanding job, then weight training could help you improve your performance, or better cope with your daily duties.

You may have already tried weight training with limited success. Common mistakes include over-training (training too heavy and too often), training with weights that are too light and using too many repetitions, or training but not eating enough of the right kinds of food to help your body recover and build muscle.

Weight training for physique

Are you at your ideal weight, but still not happy with how you look? Do you have a dress you'd like to fit in to? Are you going on a beach holiday this summer, but dreading people seeing you in a swimsuit?

Weight training can help you get the look you're aiming for.

Chapter 4 will explain how you can improve your body composition, and explain the difference between body fat and weight. You may find that as you train and start to look more 'toned' the number on the scales will go up. That isn't something to be scared of. Pay attention to the most important number – the tape measure. Once you learn to ignore the scale and focus on eating healthily and training sensibly, you will quickly notice improvements in how you look.

'Weight training can help you get the look you're aiming for.'

Weight training myths addressed

Weight training is all muscle-bound guys who will laugh at me.

Most lifters – be they bodybuilders or power lifters, are always happy to see people trying to improve their bodies. They may look intimidating while they're working out in the gym, but that's just because they're so focused on their workouts.

If you're self conscious about working out in a gym, don't be! Most people who go to the gym are so engrossed in their own workouts they won't even notice you.

Weight training with free weights is dangerous, I could injure myself.

'It's very hard for a woman to build enough muscle that they look like a man!'

All exercise comes with some risks, but free weights can actually protect you from injury, if they are used correctly. When you use weight machines, you are limited to the range of motion that the machine offers. If you are short or tall, you may find that the machine isn't suited to you, and you have to adjust your form to perform an exercise on the machine. Machines also tend to bring fewer muscle groups in to play than free weights do, so in the long term you could end up with strength imbalances that will cause problems later.

Free weights require you to control the weight through the full range of each exercise. This means more muscles are exercised. If you're already a gym member, you may find that you can squat more on a machine than you can with free weights – this isn't a bad thing! Start with light weights – many people start training with just the bar – and perfect your form before you increase the weight you are working with. If you train sensibly, your risk of injury will be minimal.

I'm a woman; I don't want to lift weights because I'll look like a man.

It's very hard for a woman to build enough muscle that they look like a man! Women have far, far lower levels of the hormones that encourage hypertrophy (muscle growth). Lifting heavy weights will make you look firmer and leaner, accentuating the right curves in your shape, you won't look bulky and masculine!

I can't get to the gym, and I don't want to clutter my house up with tons of exercise equipment.

You don't need tons of equipment to get started! A set of dumbbells will go a long way (and doesn't take up much space). Add a barbell, and you can do almost every exercise you can think of, all with equipment that can easily be stored away when not in use.

Exercise machines are convenient, but a barbell and a set of dumbbells can be used to do an almost infinite number of exercises, so your workouts need not get repetitive.

Working out is pointless if you don't take steroids.

If you're working out with the goal of losing weight, toning up, or just getting a little stronger, then eating well and training enthusiastically will offer good progress. If you want to compete as a power lifter or a bodybuilder, then you will need to approach your training more seriously, but if you look at the rules of the main British bodybuilding and power lifting federations (which are listed in Chapter Eight), you will notice that there are a huge number of Natural (Steroid free) federations.

I am vegetarian / vegan, I can't build muscle.

Protein is essential for muscle growth. It is true that vegetarians and vegans tend to have less protein in their diet than meat eaters, but it is possible for vegetarians to benefit from weight training. Famous vegetarian weight trainers include bodybuilder and four times Mr Universe Bill Pearl, and the power lifting champion Bill Manetti.

Before you begin

Before you embark on any form of fitness programme, you should consult your doctor. This is especially important if you are overweight or underweight, have any pre-existing medical conditions, or have been sedentary for a long time.

If your doctor makes any recommendations regarding your training programme, be sure to follow them. As your fitness increases, you can seek further advice and re-evaluate your training programme.

Gym Etiquette

If you don't have access to equipment at home, you can work out at a gym. The following are some simple gym etiquette tips:

- Don't hog multiple stations at once.

- Re-rack your weights when you are done.

- If someone leaves a towel on a bench, it usually means they are using it.

- Don't ask to 'work in' (share equipment) with someone if you are going to need to make massive adjustments to the weights or seat settings each set.

- If you want to talk to someone, wait until they have finished their set – they probably don't want to be distracted while they're exercising.

- Don't walk in front of the mirror if it will obscure their view while they are exercising.

- Take a towel with you, and wipe down your station when you are finished.

- Some noise is usually acceptable, but try to put your weights down gently

- If someone is listening to an MP3 player, they probably don't want to be approached.

- Don't go to the gym wearing lots of cologne or perfume – it's good to smell clean, but overpowering perfumes could interfere with other people's workouts.

Most gym etiquette is common sense – if you are considerate of other gym users, then you should have a good gym experience.

Getting Started – Gearing Up

Throughout this book, I will assume that you are exercising at home. For each body part, I will describe simple but effective exercises that can be done with just barbells and plates. I will also describe alternative exercises which can be done with a dumbbell, and which make use of a bench.

What you need:

It's possible to get started with weight training with very little equipment. The following are the most important basics:

Clothing

You don't need to rush out and buy straps, gloves, or a weight belt immediately, however you should make sure that you are dressed comfortably. At the very least, you need:

- Comfortable jogging pants or shorts – something that does not restrict your movement.
- A breathable T-Shirt – again, something that will not restrict your movement.
- Flat soled gym shoes – for stability, and to protect your feet if you drop any weight plates.

Some people like to work out barefoot, however this is forbidden at most commercial gyms, and could be dangerous if you accidentally drop a plate or dumbbell – even the plimsolls that school children wear in gym class offer a small amount of protection.

Trainers are okay for some exercises, however if you plan to squat or deadlift, you may find that the bouncy soles of certain brands of trainers will cause problems. It is better to wear flat soled shoes. Chuck Taylors are a brand that many lifters recommend, however any similar style of shoe will work. The important thing is that they fit well, and are comfortable.

'You don't need to rush out and buy straps, gloves, or a weight belt immediately.'

Exercise Equipment

At a minimum you should invest in:

- A set of adjustable dumbbells.
- Some plates.
- A roll-up exercise mat or aerobics mat.

You could also consider:

- A barbell and some more plates.

- A weight bench.

- A bosu ball.

Usually, when you buy a dumbbell set, it will come with some plates – the total weight will be listed on the box. In my experience, most beginners quickly outgrow the basic set, especially if they were moderately active before they started weight training.

You can buy extra weight plates quite cheaply. My local gym store charges less than £1 per KG for hammertone plates, and slightly more for rubber coated plates.

I take the stance that your body does not care what the weight you are lifting is made out of, so I opt for the cheaper hammertone plates. I am fortunate enough to live in house with enough room to work out downstairs, and neighbours that are out during the day so can't hear the 'thunk' of my weights!

If you are working out upstairs, or are concerned about noise, then it may be worth paying a little extra for rubber coated plates.

Weight benches come in many flavours, some have safetys, which make them good for bench pressing – although it's still a good idea to use a spotter if you have access to one. Simple collapsible benches are relatively inexpensive, and are worth investing in, as they really open up the number of exercise options you have.

Summing Up

- Weight training is a great way to get fit and feel good. The strength you gain in the gym will benefit you in other areas of your life.

- This book will give you an introduction to weight training, and will help you to learn the most important exercises, and put them together into simple programs. From there, it's up to you how you proceed. You may want to take your weight training to the next level, and compete in bodybuilding or powerlifting contests. Or, you may decide that you're just happy being strong and healthy, and train purely with the goal of staying that way. Whatever you choose, welcome to a fitter, healthier life.

Basic Exercises

I t's easy to feel intimidated the first time you walk into a gym and see the huge arrays of machines, dumbbells, and barbells. What exercises should you do? How do you use that bit of equipment? Is that exercise even safe anyway?

The good news is that you don't really need to learn and do dozens of different exercises. You can get a great workout with just a few major exercises known as 'compound lifts'. These lifts work several different muscle groups, meaning you can get fitter and stronger without spending hours in the gym.

Basic exercises

The first part of this chapter is essentially an exercise directory. Don't feel tempted to try each of these exercises one after the other! At best, you'll exhaust yourself doing a series of unrelated exercises, and at worst you could get injured by trying to do too much in one session.

At the end of this chapter you'll find a beginner's workout programme. Chapters 3 through to 6 contain more specialist workout programmes for people with more specific goals.

Upper body and arms

Overhead press

I've listed this as an upper body exercise, but in truth, the overhead press is a great full-body exercise. To get the bar from the starting position to the top of the lift you're employing your whole body. Your legs and your core need to stay balanced and stable as you push the weight up above your head. Your shoulders get a good workout from the overhead press too.

Important points

- Learn the lift with an empty bar

- Start with the bar on the rack at shoulder height. If you don't have a rack, you can press with an amount that you can clean up to your shoulders instead.

- Grip the bar so that the weight is pushing into the heel of your hand, and let the weight rest on your anterior deltoids (the fleshy part of your shoulder).

- Point your elbows forward so that they're in front of the bar when viewed from the side.

- Push the bar upwards. At the top of the movement you want to end up under the bar – do this by moving your body forward, rather than moving the bar backwards.

- Try to keep the path of the bar as straight as possible. Take are not to excessively arch (or round) your back.

Dumbbell Bench Press

The dumbbell bench press is good for targeting the Pectorialis Major, and also employs the Biceps, Triceps, and Deltoid muscles. If you have form issues when performing a barbell bench press, then using dumbbells can help, as each side is worked independently.

Start by sitting on a bench, put the dumbbells up on your shoulders, and lie back, then move the dumbbells out so that they're to the sides of your chest.

Press the dumbbells up – the dumbbell should follow a slight arch pattern. Lower the dumbbells again until you feel a slight stretch in your chest.

Important points

- The movement of the dumbbells should be slow and steady

- When you have finished the lift, don't drop the weights – you could damage the weights, or worse, injure someone that is exercising near you. Instead, bring the weights back to the starting position and then sit up, lowering the weights to your knees as you do so.

Barbell bench press

The bench press is a popular exercise, and one of the 'big three' used in power lifting competitions. The bench press works the Pectorialis Major, and also employs the biceps, triceps, and deltoid muscles.

Begin by lying down on the bench in a natural position. You should have a slight arch to your spine, but not an extreme one.

To find the right grip, put your arms out toy our side, bend your elbows, and then grip the bar. The bar should be positioned over the heel of your hand.

Unrack the bar and move it out so that it is over your chest. Inhale, then lower the bar to your chest. When the bar touches your chest, exhale and push the bar up.

Important points

- Make sure your thumb is wrapped around the bar. Do not ever use a thumbless grip.

- As with all exercises, start with the bar, then gradually add weight

- Never bench press without a spotter

Dumbbell Flye

Holding the two dumbbells, lie on the bench. Support dumbbells above your chest with your arms fixed in a slightly bent position, with your elbows pointing outwards.

Lower the dumbbells to your sides until you can feel a slight stretch in your chest. Try to keep your elbows bent at all times.

Bring your arms upwards until the dumbbells are almost touching each other, then lower them to your sides again.

It is important that the motion/rotation comes from your shoulders (not your wrists). Your elbows should be pointing outwards at the top of the motion, and downwards at the bottom of the motion.

Bicep Curl

The biceps curl should be fairly self explanatory. Raise and lower the dumbbell in a slow, controlled fashion. Do not be tempted to rock back and forth with the motion – the dumbbell should be in control at all points in the movement.

Overhead Triceps Extensions

Position the dumbbell overhead with your hand near the inner plate. Lower your forearm behind your upper arm by flexing at the elbow (also flex your wrist, so that you don't hit yourself in the neck!). Raise the dumbbell overhead, slowly lower again, and repeat.

You will need to use a light weight for this exercise. You can increase the weight slightly by using a two-handed grip instead of one hand, but you will need to take care to avoid hitting yourself in the head. Some people refer to this exercise as the 'Skullcrusher' – be careful you don't do that to yourself!

Shoulder Press

Lift the dumbbells up to your shoulder, palms in. Raise the dumbbells up above your head. Take care not to arch your back while doing so. Breathe in while lowering the dumbbells, and out while raising them.

Front Raise

Hold the dumbbells by your side, and then raise your arms out in front of you. Keep a steady tension in your arms and wrists. Take care not to lean back, and not to 'swing' the dumbbells up. This should be a controlled movement. Hold for a few seconds at the top of the movement, then lower the dumbbells again slowly.

Single Arm Row

Rest one leg on a box or your bench, bend over, but try to keep your spine in a fairly neutral position.

Lower your arm while grasping the dumbbell, and then raise your arm, keeping your elbows in. Repeat.

Row

Begin by holding the dumbbells so that your palms are facing towards your thighs. Raise the dumbbells up to the front of the shoulder. Try to keep your elbows in, and don't raise your arms too high.

Allow your wrists to flex slightly at the top of the motion.

Legs

Barbell Squat

Face the squat rack, and step under the bar, position the bar high on your back, across your shoulders. Grip the bar as shown in the diagram (note that the thumbs do not wrap around the bar).

Carefully unrack the bar. Take care to keep your shoulders back and head up – looking at a fixed point on the wall will help with this.

Position your feet slightly more than shoulder-width apart, with the toes pointing slightly outwards. Squat down by bending your knees whilst also creasing at the hips – you should feel like you are attempting to sit back into the squat.

Descend until the crease of your hip is slightly lower than the top of the knee, then stand back up – try to raise your head before your legs. If your legs start coming up first, then your back straightens afterwards, then lower the weight until you get the correct form sorted.

You may have heard some people say that squatting below parallel is bad for the knees, but this is not true. When performed correctly, a below parallel squat is safer – by bending your knees further, you are activating the muscles in the glutes, which actually reduces stress on the knees.

The important thing is to perform the exercise correctly. If your back is bending, or your knees collapse inwards when you're squatting, you could be at risk of injuring yourself. It's better to do correct squats with just the bar (or even bodyweight squats), than it is to use a heavier weight but perform only partial squats, or squats with bad form.

Lunges

Stand with dumbbells held by your side.

Lunge forward with one leg, landing on your heel then fore-foot. Lower your body by flexing the knee and hip of your front leg. When the knee of the rear leg touches the floor, stand up using your front leg. Repeat the same process with the opposite leg.

Split Squat

Hold dumbbells as you would for a lunge. Rest the foot / shin of your rear leg on a box or your weight bench. Squat down using the front leg, then stand back up. The rear leg should not be taking much weight – just used for balance.

Back

Deadlift

There are two ways to perform a deadlift. Sumo stance, and conventional stance. The stance described below is Sumo stance.

Stand with your feet wide apart. Position the barbell so that it is very close to your shins. Grip the barbell with an overhand grip, and squat down low. Lift the barbell off the floor by extending your hips, then your knees. At the top of the lift, pull your shoulders back if they have rounded.

The lift should come from your hips, glutes, and knees. Your knees should always be pointed forwards, and you should try to make sure that your back does not round at any point in the lift.

If you have problems with the overhand grip, try a mixed grip (one hand over, one hand under). If you use mixed grip, alternate your hands each session so that both hands develop grip strength in the same way.

The traditional deadlift stance is narrower than sumo stance, and the grip is placed outside the legs. Many people find they can lift heavier weights with traditional stance, however in my experience female lifters usually find sumo more suitable for their proportions.

Goodmorning

The goodmorning is a useful hamstring exercise, but care must be taken to perform it correctly.

Begin by positioning the barbell on the back of your shoulders. Hold the bar on both sides as you would for a squat, but with the thumb wrapped around the bar.

Keeping your back straight, bend your hips until your torso is parallel to the floor (or until you feel a mild stretch in your hamstrings), and then raise your torso back up to standing position.

It is vital that you begin this exercise with very light weights, and add weight slowly.

need2know

Bodyweight exercises

Triangle push up

Get into a push-up position, but instead of having your hands shoulder-width apart, position them close together, so that your fingers and thumbs meet to form a triangle. Keeping your core tight and your back straight, lower yourself to the ground until your head touches your hands, then raise yourself back up into the push-up position.

Side plank

Lie on your side with one arm on the floor, raise your hips until you are in the position shown below. Hold this position for the desired length of the exercise.

If you have difficulty holding the position with your arm fully extended, try the modified side plank, which uses a bent arm.

Modified side plank

As with the plank, begin by lying on your side. The main difference is that you start with the supporting arm bent, and the forearm pointing perpendicular to your body. Raise your body by straightening your waist. You can add weight to the exercise, or hold it for longer, as you get stronger.

Twisting sit up

Lie down with your knees bent. Raise your arms – you can place them lightly behind your head, but do not pull on your head or neck as you come up. Just rest them lightly behind your head.

Sit up, and as you do so, twist your body so that your right elbow touches your left leg. Slowly sit back down, then repeat the motion, twisting in the other direction.

Superman

Lie flat on the floor with your arms extended in front of you. Raise your arms and legs off the floor, slowly. Then slowly lower your arms and legs for one repetition.

This exercise is designed to be performed slowly. Jerking, fast movements will not produce full benefit.

Plyometrics

Plyometric exercises involve explosive movements. They are a key part of many sports, and on top of that offer a great workout.

Explosive Squat

Squat down with your arms in front of you until your finger tips touch the ground. Then jump up, exploding out of the squatting position with as much speed and power as you can manage.

Burpees

Begin in a squatting position with your hands on the ground in front of you. Kick your legs backwards into a position similar to a push-up. Then jump your legs back into the original starting position. Finally, explode up into standing position. For added intensity, do a star-jump while standing before performing another repetition.

Burpees should be performed as fast as you can manage them.

Chops

Chops are often referred to as woodcutters. They are so named because of the wood chopping motion that is used. They are usually performed with either a kettlebell or a medicine ball, but a weight plate with handles is suitable too.

Hold your chosen weight securely, place your feet wide apart, pointing slightly outwards. Bend your knees slightly. Raise the weight to the side of your head, with your arms bent. Bring the weight downward, diagonally in front of you, while rotating your hip. Then swing the weight back to the side of your head.

When you have finished your repetitions, repeat the exercise with the weight starting on the opposite side of your body.

Summing Up

- This chapter covered several different exercises. You would not use all of these exercises in one workout, though! Remember to start all of these exercises with low weights (ideally, just the bar), and work up gradually as you gain confidence, strength, and the ability to perform them correctly.

- The next chapter will describe a simple programme that makes use of the core exercises. You can add other exercises depending on the parts of your body that you want to focus on, or the needs of your chosen sport.

3

Weight Training for Fat Loss

For many people, the biggest motivator for going to the gym is a desire to look good on the beach, fit into a nice new outfit, or just shed a few pounds of fat for health reasons. Weight training is a great way to do this while escaping the monotony of the elliptical, treadmill, or exercise bike.

Weight vs. Fat – Why weighing more isn't always bad

When it comes to starting a new diet and exercise regimen, the bathroom scales can be your worst enemy. There's two reasons for this:

Scales can kill motivation

It's common, in the first week or two of a new diet, to see massive weight loss – but that weight loss isn't all from fat. When you clean up your diet and start exercising, you can lose a lot of water weight. Even if you're aware of that, it's easy to feel down when the next week, your losses are much lower.

Muscle is denser than fat

If you're fairly close to your goal physique, and just want to 'tone' then you may find that as you lose inches and start looking how you want to look, the scales either don't move, or go up slightly. This is because you're losing fat, but gaining muscle. It's natural to worry when you see the scale go in what you think is the wrong direction, but take a look in the mirror – if you see a slimmer, firmer version of yourself, keep doing what you're doing!

But I don't want to get muscular!

One common concern is fear of getting too bulky. This was already mentioned in Chapter 1, but it bears repeating. You can't turn into a bodybuilder by accident! Weight training, when coupled with a diet geared towards gradual weight loss, will not only burn Calories while you're doing it, it will boost your metabolism for a long time afterwards – a study published in the European Journal of Applied Physiology (Jan 29 2002; 86(5):411 – 7) showed that weight training can increase the trainee's metabolism for up to 38 hours post workout.

That's not to say that cardio is bad – indeed cardio does have a similar (but not quite as long lasting) 'after burn' effect. However, weight training encourages your body to hold on to its lean muscle – and muscle is a big help when it comes to burning Calories, and losing fat.

How fast can results be expected?

Sustainable weight loss isn't something that can be achieved overnight. The closer you are to your ideal weight, the slower weight loss becomes. If you want to lose fat whilst retaining muscle (ensuring that you'll be able to keep the weight off long term), then you'll need to set reasonable expectations in terms of how much weight you lose each month.

As a guideline, if you are:

- Obese: 6-8%
- Moderately overweight: 4-6%
- Average weight: 2-4%
- Lean: 1-2%
- Very lean: 0.5 – 1%

These percentages are the amount of scale weight you would be aiming to lose in order to reduce fat without losing too much muscle. That means that if you weigh 200lbs, you can expect to lose 12 – 16lbs a month (or 3-4lbs a week). As you get closer to your ideal weight, that figure can drop to as little as 1lb a month. That might not sound as impressive as the stories you read about in magazines and on TV, but this is the healthy way to do it, and the way to end up with a firm 'toned' looking physique, instead of just looking a bit smaller, but keeping your problem areas.

Calculating your Calorie requirements

At its most basic level, weight loss occurs when your body uses more Calories than you consume in a day. It's this knowledge that leads many people to try crash diets – consuming far fewer Calories than they need in the hopes of seeing fat literally melt off.

Crash diets, however, don't work in the long term. When you starve yourself, your body doesn't just turn to fat for energy, it also consumes muscle. So, instead of looking lean and toned at the end of your diet, you feel weaker, and while you look smaller, you won't have gained the beach body you're hoping for – you'll still look 'soft' or even 'flabby' because you've lost a lot of muscle, as well as fat.

In addition, by losing muscle, you slow your metabolism down. So, your body needs fewer Calories to maintain its weight. When your eating habits return to normal, you'll quickly find that you put weight back on.

If you want to lose weight and keep it off, you need to aim for slow, sustainable weight loss. This means figuring out the amount of Calories you need for a day, and eating just under that level.

To figure out how many Calories you need per day, use the following formula (the Katch-McArdle formula):

BMR = (9.99 x weight (kg)) + (6.25 x height (cm)) – (4.92 x age (years)) -161

The above gives you your base metabolic rate. That is the number of Calories you would use in a day if you stayed in bed all day. Of course, most people get out of bed and do something during the day – even if it's just drive to work and sit in an office chair for eight hours. Just sitting at a desk uses some Calories, so we need to factor that in.

Take your BMR and multiply that by one of the following values, as appropriate:

Multiply By	Activity Level
1.2	Sedentary (office job, no activity)
1.3 – 1.4	Lightly active (gentle exercise 1-3 times a week)
1.5 – 1.6	Moderately active (Moderate exercise 3-5 times per week)
1.6 – 1.7	Very active (physical job, sports 6-7 times a week)
1.8 – 1.9	Extremely active (Hard daily exercise, manual labour based job)
The above factors include work, sport, and assume an 'average' diet.	

Try to be honest when working out your lifestyle. A common mistake is to overestimate the amount of activity you do. If you work in an office, and go to the gym three times a week, play it safe and put yourself in the 'Lightly active' category, rather than 'Moderately active'.

If the above formula gives you a headache, you can use the following website to get an estimate: **http://www.exrx.net/Calculators/CalRequire.html**

Deciding your daily allowances

Now that you know the number of Calories that you need to eat per day to maintain your weight, you can start thinking about your daily food intake.

If you want to lose weight, take your daily Calorie allowance, and subtract 15% from it. The number you get is the number of Calories you should aim for per day.

So, if your daily Calorie allowance is 1,500 and you want to lose weight, then you would aim for 1275 Calories per day (1,500 x 0.85).

To lose 1lb of bodyweight (which could be fat or muscle), you need to burn around 3,500 Calories more than you consume, so if you ate at a 225 Calorie deficit, you'd be looking at a weight loss rate of around 2lbs a month. That's slow, but easily sustainable.

The example above is someone with a fairly small Calorie allowance, so they are probably fairly small, and don't have a lot of weight to lose. Someone with more weight to lose would have a bigger Calorie allowance, and therefore lose weight more quickly if they ate at a 15% deficit.

More than just Calories

Now that we've worked out the Calorie allowance, let's think about how to use those Calories.

It's all too easy to make the mistake of trying to live off salads while on a diet. That won't do you much good in the long run! An ideal diet should include a mixture of proteins, carbohydrates and healthy fats. Yes, fats are not the bad guy! You need some fats to stay healthy.

The following rules of thumb are a good idea to work towards:

- Protein: 1.2 – 1.6g of protein per KG of bodyweight
- Fats: 1-2g fat / KG bodyweight for someone lose to their ideal weight. Aim for 1g fat / KG bodyweight if you have a high body fat percentage.
- Carbohydrates: There are no specific 'requirements' for Carbohydrates, but it's a good idea to try to eat some complex carbohydrates (oats, wholemeal bread, etc) each day.

Carbohydrates are not the 'bad guy', and neither are fats. They are targeted by a lot of diets because they are Calorie dense foods – it's easier to eat a low Calorie diet if you cut out anything that contains a lot of Calories, but doesn't fill you up!

The above figures are suggestions for a healthy adult. Adolescents, the elderly, and people with pre-existing medical conditions, may have different requirements and should consult their doctor before making drastic changes to their diet.

Making healthy food choices

Any diet that is going to help you achieve sustainable weight loss will be a personal thing. There's not much point pushing specific rules such as 'Always eat breakfast', or 'No carbs after 6PM' – those strategies may not be appropriate for your lifestyle.

'To lose 1lb of bodyweight (which could be fat or muscle), you need to burn around 3,500 Calories more than you consume, so if you ate at a 225 Calorie deficit, you'd be looking at a weight loss rate of around 2lbs a month.'

If eating breakfast stops you snacking on Calorie dense, nutritionally void snacks during the day, then do so. If eating breakfast makes you feel sick on the commute into work, don't bother.

The important thing is to make sure that you eat a balanced and varied diet. Some people find that the only way that they can stick to their Calorie requirement is to cut out all sugary snacks and treats. Other people find that limiting snacks works better than cutting them out entirely.

One popular strategy is to follow a fairly strict diet most of the time, but to designate one or two days each month which are 'cheat' days, or 'refeeds'. On those days you treat yourself – perhaps going out for a Pizza, or having chocolate cake with your evening meal. If that gives you something to look forward to, and helps with willpower, then it sounds like a good plan to me!

Simple changes

The mantra for this chapter is 'sustainable'. Completely changing your eating habits, and cutting out all your favourite foods probably won't work in the long run. Small changes, however, are a lot easier to stick to.

For example, you could:

- Reduce the amount of sugar you take in your tea by one spoonful.
- Swap whole milk for semi-skimmed.
- Swap chips for a jacket potato or brown rice.
- Swap chocolate biscuits for oatcakes.
- Have porridge oats instead of sugary cereal.
- Swap white bread for wholemeal.
- Drink water instead of cola.
- Use a smaller plate at meal times to reduce overall portion size.
- Stop ordering starters when you eat out at restaurants.
- Stop having dressing on your salads, and don't order extra cheese.

The above are just a few suggestions. If you stop to write down everything you eat for a day or two, you'll be amazed at where all your Calories are going. Soda, beer, and sugar in drinks such as tea and coffee can make a massive dent in your daily Calorie allowance! You may find that it's not what you eat that's been making you gain weight, but what you drink!

Track everything

If you've tried dieting in the past, but without much success, it could be that you're missing out on little things – such as Calories from drinks, or from the chocolates that get passed around the office almost every day because there's inevitably a birthday, promotion, or leaving celebration.

It's easier than ever to track your Calorie intake and physical activity level. Tools such as the fitness and exercise diaries at **www.weightlossresources.co.uk** and Fitday (**www. fitday.com**), and the excellent Cardio Trainer app for Android phones, or RunKeeper for both Android and the iPhone, allow you to track everything you do. When you know exactly what you're eating, and exactly what you're burning, it's easy to keep track of your progress.

'Use a smaller plate at meal times to reduce overall portion size.'

Weight training for weight loss

Cardiovascular exercise is useful for losing weight, but weight training is valuable too. Cardiovascular exercise burns Calories while you're doing it, and also elevates your metabolic rate for a short time afterwards. The benefit of weight training is more subtle, but still valuable.

The US National Council on Strength & Fitness estimates that 1lb of muscle burns 6 Calories/day just by existing. That's before exercise, or even day to day bodily functions, are taken into account. Weight training encourages your body to build more muscle, which means that you're encouraging your body to use more Calories – hopefully accelerating weight loss.

High Reps or Low Reps?

Conventional wisdom used to dictate that people would lift heavy weights for a low number of repetitions to get strong, and use lighter weights for more repetitions to get lean.

While it's true that lifting heavy weights for low repetitions builds strength, you don't have to go to the opposite end of the scale to lose weight. The best idea is to select weights that you find challenging when lifting in the 6-8 repetition range, and use those for your weight training.

Which exercises?

The best exercises for weight loss are ones that employ the whole body. These are known as 'Compound' exercises. The squat and the deadlift are good examples. If you want to add in some cardio after you're done with your weight training, then go for it. Just make sure that you train hard in the weights section of your workout.

Below is an example program to help you get started. You can find more program suggestions under the Books category at **www.geeks-in-gis.com**.

Workout A

Exercises	Reps
Squat (heavy weight)	3 x 5
Bench	3 x 5
Barbell Row	3 x 5
Triceps Kickbacks	3 x 8
Cardio	15 – 30mins of your choice

Workout B

Exercise	Reps
Lunges	3 x 10
Overhead Press	3 x 5
Deadlift	1 x 5
Pushups	2 x 20 (or until failure)
Supermans/Goodmornings (for more advanced workouts)	2 x 8

Workout C

Exercise	Reps
Squat (lighter weight)	3 x 8
Lateral Raise	3 x 8 (hold each repetition for a count of 5)
Deadlift	1 x 5
Barbell Row	3 x 5
Crunches	2 x 20
Burpees	2 x 20 (complete as fast as possible)

Remember to spend at least five minutes warming up before you start the above exercises. Also, the sets/repetitions listed above are for your working set. Before you attempt the full weight, start with the bar, and add a few KG at a time to work up to the working set. This does mean that the workout takes longer, but it will reduce your risk of injury. Oh, and it means you get to move more weight, which burns more Calories!

Beach bodies are made in the kitchen

'You can't out-train a bad diet.'

Weight training will make you stronger, improve your metabolism, and hopefully protect you from injury and give you more energy, but if your diet isn't good then you will lose out on the benefits of the exercise. You can't out-train a bad diet.

This contains some basic information to get you started on the road to a healthy diet, but the long term work is something that you will have to do alone.

Summing Up

- This chapter covered a few basic points for weight training with the goal of losing fat. Before you start training, it's a good idea to speak to your doctor. This is important for everyone, but it's especially true if you've been sedentary for a while or have more than just a few pounds to lose.

- Remember that being fit is a lifestyle, not a short term thing. The program suggested here is a steady, sustainable one. It's easy to get over-enthusiastic when you're just starting out and be tempted to go even lower on Calories, or train more days a week, or add more exercises – but that is likely to lead to disaster in the long term.

- Take it slow, train safe, and above all, enjoy the benefits of your new found lifestyle. If you do, you'll be reaping those benefits for many years to come!

4

Weight Training for Physique

The two biggest motivators that encourage most people to get into shape are health, and physique. Getting in shape for the summer, or for a special event such as a wedding or a big holiday can be a big motivator. Even better, once you've enjoyed that big event and seen how great you look, you'll be motivated to make a long term lifestyle change.

Weights vs. Cardio

If you're close to your ideal weight, then changing your physique can be challenging. When you have a lot of fat to lose, it's easy to do so by eating at a slight Calorie deficit (as described in Chapter 3), and increasing your overall activity level. As you get closer to your correct weight on the scales, you may find that weight loss slows down. You may also find that while you're a lot happier with the number that the scales report, you still don't like how you look.

This is where weight training comes in. Weight training will encourage your body to build muscle – or, if you're eating at a slight deficit, to hold on to the muscle that you already have. So, instead of your body using muscle and fat for fuel, the focus will be shifted more towards fat burning, and you'll end up looking firmer, and more toned.

Jargon busted

The 'toned' look that so many people desire can be obtained in a number of ways, and if you spend any length of time in a gym you may hear people discussing the different ways of shaping your body. Some people like to make changes gradually, while others have cycles of gaining muscle (and some fat with it), and then dieting to lose the fat, revealing a great physique underneath.

These different styles are called, recomping, bulking, and cutting.

Recomping

Recomping involves losing body fat while attempting to gain muscle. It's this practice which leads some people to say that they are going to 'turn fat into muscle', but that's not really what happens. Recomping is a slow process, but it is great for people who don't want to go through the bulking phase.

Bulking

Bulking involves eating over maintenance (see Chapter 3 for details about calculating your maintenance Calorie needs), while engaging in regular strength training. Bulking involves gaining weight, some of which will be fat. For this reason, it is rare to see anyone who is not a weight class athlete or a bodybuilder engage in this practice.

Cutting

The cutting phase usually follows the bulking phase. This is where most fat loss occurs. Cutting involves eating at a Calorie deficit. During this phase, your energy levels may drop, and your intensity in the gym may suffer. It's common for people to lift lighter weights than normal while they are cutting – but that is not because lifting light weights helps the cut, it's simply because they don't have the energy that they had while they were bulking.

The idea of 'high weights, low reps for getting big muscles and low weights, high reps to get toned' comes more from this practice, and is rather misleading. When you're cutting (or recomping), you still need to lift weights that feel heavy to you. You may find that 'heavy' is 5lbs lighter when you're eating below maintenance, but it still needs to feel heavy!

A Sample Training Program

The following program suggestion is not a standard three day split, but the exercises have been grouped together so that the focus is mostly on one area of the body each workout. The split squats were added to Wednesday because many people find it hard to do traditional squats twice a week – especially once they reach an intermediate level of lifting, and are squatting with heavier weights.

Monday

- Dumbbell Bench Press
- Front Raise
- Lateral Raises
- Overhead Press
- Dumbbell Rows

Wednesday

- Split Squats
- Barbell Rows
- Shoulder Press
- Bicep Curl / Hammer Curl
- Deadlifts

Friday

- Squats

- Lunges

- Calf Raises

- Crunches (weighted if required)

For each of these exercises, follow the advice given in Chapter 2 (to recap, start with just the bar for barbell exercises, and a light weight for dumbbells. Increase the weight gradually, until you reach your working set, and do that for three sets of five repetitions). Try to keep the rest periods between each set fairly short. If you are training at full intensity and find you need a long time between sets, then consider decreasing the weight slightly.

You can find spreadsheets to help calculate the weight intervals/increases for these workouts in the Programmes section of www.geeks-in-gis.com

In addition to the three days of weight training, try to fit in two cardio sessions each week.

The programme above is designed with short but fairly intense workouts in mind. You shouldn't need to spend more than an hour in the gym each night, and the cardio suggestions given below are designed around 30 minute workouts.

'If you're looking for something more exotic (and a lot of fun!) think about Tabatta.'

Cardio ideas

Getting that perfect physique can be challenging. When you are nearing your goal weight, it is a good idea to eat at around maintenance, and slightly increase your activity level. This does not mean spending hours on a cardio machine, but some extra cardio training can be beneficial.

Rather than lot of Low Intensity Steady Speed cardio (LISS), why not try High Intensity Interval Training (HIIT). This kind of training involves short bursts of activity, followed by intervals of less intense training. One example could be sprinting on a treadmill for a short time, followed by a few minutes of walking, then more sprinting.

Another option, if you're looking for something more exotic (and a lot of fun!) is Tabatta. A tabatta workout is pretty short – with most lasting around 16 minutes, but they are intense, and have a lot of variety.

In a tabatta workout, you exercise at maximum effort for 20 seconds, rest for 10 seconds, then exercise again, for example:

- Push ups

- Sit ups

- Jump rope

- Bodyweight squats

- Sprint up and down the gym

- Plyo Squats

- Triangle Push Ups

- Burpees

If you work through the above cycle of exercises (20 seconds each, with a 10 second rest in between), twice, then you have a basic tabatta workout. It doesn't take long to do, but you'll be tired afterwards (in a good way!).

Some people like to add heavy bag punching / kicking work into a tabatta workout. If you enjoy kickboxing or boxercise then that's a great idea. You could also do step-aerobics type exercises. The important thing with tabatta is that you do exercises that you enjoy, and that you keep moving during those 20 second bouts.

Diet

The advice given in Chapter 3 applies here. If you've been dieting for a while, and are now approaching your goal weight, then now is a good time to re-evaluate your maintenance Calorie levels. One common mistake that people make at this point is to eat too little, which is counterproductive. Make sure you're eating enough to keep your energy levels high!

Tracking your progress

The closer you get to your ideal weight, the less important the scale becomes. If you find this difficult to accept, just take a look at some of the stats of the Fitness and Bikini models that compete in shows with federations such as the UKBFF and NABBA (or American federations such as NPC). The competitors in the non Bodybuilding classes are lean and toned, and look like they have a far lower scale weight than they really do.

The best way to track your progress is to leave the scales, and use a combination of the tape measure, regular progress photos, and bodyfat measurement. These indicators combined will give you an idea of how you're getting on.

Why progress photos?

You see yourself in the mirror every day. The closer you get to your goal physique, the longer it takes to see changes. The changes that do happen are subtle ones, and they're easy to miss. Over time those subtle improvements build up, but to your own eye the changes have been so small that you don't realise how far you've come.

Progress photos allow you to look back at your work over the past few months, objectively. They're a great motivator, and, if you ever choose to share them, a great inspiration for people looking to follow in your footsteps.

'Progress photos allow you to look back at your work over the past few months, objectively.'

Bodyfat Measurement

Bodyfat measuring tools are a tricky area. The tools that you can use in your own home – for example digital scales, and bodyfat callipers, aren't exactly accurate. The scales are extremely sensitive to hydration levels – so even a cup of coffee can massively alter the readings. Callipers are accurate in the hands of a trained person, but can give unreliable readings if the person who measures you is inexperienced.

With that said, I still think that bodyfat measuring is good for tracking progress. If you choose to use bodyfat measuring scales, then try to always weigh yourself at the same time of the day, every day. If you use callipers, then try to get the same person to measure you each time. Some callipers come with a 'single point' chart that you can use if you want to measure your own bodyfat, and that's fine for a general idea if you can't find someone willing to do a full test for you.

Ideally, though, you should aim for a four point test (or even better, seven point), done by the same person each time.

The chart below is for a four-point calliper test. It's not perfect, because it doesn't test the amount of bodyfat you carry on your legs, but it's good for a general guide. If your measurements are going down, you're making progress. If, over the course of three or four tests, you see a trend that the number is increasing, then you probably need to re-evaluate your diet or switch up your training program.

The four points used for the following bodyfat test are:

- Triceps – halfway between the top of the arm and the elbow, at the rear of the arm. Take a vertical skin-fold measurement at this point

- Biceps – as with the triceps measurement, except at the front of the arm

- Shoulder Blade (subscapular) – take a skin fold running out and down at an angle of 45 degrees from the bottom of the shoulder blade.

- Waist (suprailiac) – take a skin fold running horizontally across the top of the hip. The fold should be taken from a point about one inch above the protruding part of the hip bone.

Each point should give a measurement in mm. Add up all the measurements, and compare them with the following table.

Total (mm)	Age < 19	30 – 49	50+
14	9.4	14.1	17.0
16	11.2	15.7	18.6
18	12.7	17.1	20.1
20	14.1	18.4	21.4
22	15.4	19.5	22.6
24	16.5	20.6	23.7
26	17.6	21.5	24.8
28	18.6	22.4	25.7
30	19.5	23.3	26.6
35	21.6	25.2	28.6
40	23.4	26.8	30.3
45	25.0	28.3	31.9
50	26.5	28.3	31.9
55	27.8	30.8	34.6
60	29.1	31.9	35.7
65	30.2	32.9	36.7

The previous chart is designed for use by adult women. Men will need to use a different chart. There are many formulas for calculating bodyfat percentages. The above chart assumes that you are healthy, and follow a 'normal' lifestyle. If you are an athlete, then the chart may miscalculate your bodyfat percentage.

The American Council on Exercise separates different bodyfat percentages into the following categories:

Classification	Female	Male
Essential fat	10-12%	2-4%
Athletic	14-20%	6-13%
Fitness	21-24%	14-17%
Average	25-31%	18-25%
Obese	>32%	>25%

Summing Up

- Changing your physique is a long-term proposition. Rather than 'going on a diet', you are changing your lifestyle for the long term. Over time, you may find that your goals change. It's a good idea to focus on feeling healthy, and being happy with how you look, rather than obsessing with a number on the scale.

- While living a healthy lifestyle is important, remember not to put too much pressure on yourself. It's easy to get carried away measuring and counting everything – especially if you're seeing good results! Try to remember that weight training is supposed to be fun, and that you should leave room in your life for other things too. There's no point getting that great beach body if you aren't going to give yourself the time and freedom to enjoy it.

5

Weight Training for Sport

t's easy to assume that if you already take part in a sport, then you don't need to do weight training. After all, you're already active several times a week, right?

While it's true that your sports training will be doing you a lot of good health wise, it's likely that weight training would be a massive help to your sporting performance. Weight training not only makes you stronger, it can give you more explosive power (useful for many team sports), improve your stamina, protect you from injury, and make you faster.

The different kinds of strength training

One concern that many athletes have is that weight training will make them slower. This misconception comes from the fact that there are several different approaches to strength training:

- Basic strength
- Hypertrophy
- Maximal strength
- Explosive power
- Endurance training

The training outlined in the first few chapters of this book aims at basic strength – working as many body parts as possible using compound movements. The goal of basic strength training is to build a strength base – giving you a full body workout so that you're not likely to injure yourself in future training.

Hypertrophy is what bodybuilders work towards – building bigger muscles. If you're a weight class athlete, or take part in a sport that requires speed or endurance, then having a large amount of lean body mass can be a hindrance. That's not to say that bodybuilders aren't strong, but they train (and diet) with the goal of sculpting their bodies, rather than to improve their performance in a sport. They train muscles via isolation – rather than training a movement which mirrors an action in a sport.

Maximal strength training is useful for many sports – if you need to be able to kick, jump, throw, or even just run fast, then you'll benefit from building a lot of strength – especially in movements that are used in your sport.

Explosive power comes next. You need to be strong in order to develop explosive power. Once you've built up a good strength base you can focus on converting that strength into the movements that you use in your sport. For example, I have strong legs, but learning a new kick in Karate still takes time because it's a new movement. Once I've learned the technique, the strength comes into play. Karate Kumite (sparring) bouts are fairly short, and require bursts of explosive effort, so I focus on explosive power – maximum effort for short periods of time.

While explosive power is important for people who compete in sports that rely on short bursts of effort, Endurance training is important for sports with longer matches. If you'll be playing tennis or basketball, doing a triathlon, or swimming long distances, then you'll want to get your muscles used to working at moderate effort for a long time. This is where strength comes in. The stronger you are, the less perceived effort is required to perform the actions of your sport – so the easier, in theory, those actions should be to perform for the duration of a race or a match.

Planning your training

If you already practice a sport, you probably train at least a couple of times a week. It's a good idea to speak to your coach before adding any more training. Your coach knows what you are doing, and what his training plans are, and will be able to give you advice specific to your situation.

Assuming your coach gives you the go-ahead, the first thing you'll need to do is work out when to train.

Here's an example training schedule for a martial artist:

- Monday/Wed – Martial art specific training (intense cardio, bodyweight exercises, sparring)
- Tuseday/Saturday – Heavy strength training. Compound lifts.
- Thursday – Strength training, lighter weights. Tabatta / skills drills.
- Friday – Martial art specific training (light cardio, technical work)
- Sunday – Rest.

'The emphasis that your training will take depends on your sport, and the time of year.'

This schedule assumes that you're only able to work out once a day. It has one full day of rest, and two days where the emphasis is on skills rather than intense cardio or lifting. This ensures that there's plenty time for recovery.

The schedule could be adapted to focus on other things in the week running up to a competition:

Deciding the emphasis of training

The emphasis that your training will take depends on your sport, and the time of year. For example, a basketball player wouldn't want to be maxing out on strength training during the competitive season, and a swimmer wouldn't want to be doing high volume work just before a race.

Their training schedules would probably look like the example overleaf:

Swimmer

Sept	Oct	Nov	Dec	Jan	Feb	Mar	Apr	May	Jul	Jul	Aug
Off Season / Preparation				Competitions		Training		Competitions			Season End
Basic strength	Max strength	Sport specific Endurance Training		Maintenance strength training		Basic Strength	Max Strength / Endurance	Maintenance Strength training			Rest and recovery / basic strength

Martial Artist

Sept	Oct	Nov	Dec	Jan	Feb	Mar	Apr	May	Jul	Jul	Aug
Off Season				Prep	Fight	Rest / Prep	Fight	Rest/ Prep			Fight
Basic strength	Max strength	Sport specific Power training		Maint/ strength training	Active recovery		Sport specific power and endurance training	Active recovery then power/ endurance training	Maintain strength / endurance		

Team sport – e.g. basketball

Sept	Oct	Nov	Dec	Jan	Feb	Mar	Apr	May	Jul	Jul	Aug
Off Season / Preparation				Competitions Training				Competitions		Season End	
Basic strength	Hyper-trophy or Max strength	Sport specific Endurance Training		Maintenance strength training (maintain strength and power)						Rest and recovery / basic strength	

More than just training

While it's true that being stronger will help with most pursuits, there's a lot of other things to consider with sports. Strength, explosive power, speed, and skills are all important.

If you are thinking of integrating weight training into your current sports practice regime, then there are several things you need to consider:

- Does my training regime allow enough time for recovery?
- Are there other areas of training I should be focusing on right now?
- Am I building strength in the right muscles?
- How will this affect my diet?

The first point, recovery, is especially important considering you're training for a sport. Both you and your coach would be pretty disappointed if you got over-enthusiastic with your training and injured yourself before a bit game or tournament. Recovery time is needed to let your body repair itself after the rigours of training. Remember, strength gains come while you're resting – and some recovery time can help with skill performance too.

Strength training can help someone who is sedentary to get up-to-speed with the basic requirements for a new sport, but if you're already fit then you should make sure that you are getting enough sport specific training. For example, in the weeks coming up to a Karate Kata tournament, you wouldn't focus on leg strength at the expense of actually perfecting your Kata. It is true that strong legs will help you to perform better jumps and kicks – but there's no point kicking like a Black Belt if you can't even remember all the movements that go into the Kata you need to perform!

Only you and your coach will know which exercises are beneficial and which will hinder you. For a few examples:

'Recovery, is **especially important** considering you're training for a sport.'

Karate and other striking martial arts

Squatting can help to improve the power of your kicks – but make sure that you do other leg exercises too. I vary the stance of my squats (e.g. do power lifting squats, and hack squats) to ensure that all the muscles used in Karate are developed when I train.

Some people like to use weights while training – e.g. punching while holding a dumbbell, or kicking with ankle weights on. In my opinion (and the opinion of my Sensei), this is a bad idea – or at least one that should be done with caution. The risk is that you train yourself to punch with the weight – and when the weight is no-longer there you may still want to compensate for it, leading to your punches and kicks coming out high. In a grading, that could lead to you losing points and failing. In a tournament or sparring match, the consequences could be much more serious.

Most other exercises can be really beneficial for Karate. Bodyweight exercises in particular will train the hard to reach spots. There are lots of pushup variations (a few of them were listed in Chapter 2), and if you master them all you'll have a good base to work from for Karate. Tricep, shoulder, and core exercises are also useful.

Tennis

Tennis players often encounter problems with their shoulders and elbows as their career goes on. Over-use injuries can usually be alleviated through weight training. Tennis players should consider grip training and forearm exercises using light weights, and shoulder exercises with either dumbbells or resistance bands.

Lateral raises, dumbbell flyes, and overhead press are useful exercises that could help tennis players.

Dancers

Flexibility is important for dancers, but so is core strength. Deadlifts, squats, pushups, planks, and plyometric movements are all useful for dancers. Building strength can often improve flexibility, so don't be afraid of a full-body workout.

Endurance sports

One common misconception with endurance athletes is that having more muscle is always a bad thing. While it's true that you don't often see power lifters that can run for miles, that doesn't make strength training automatically a bad thing for endurance athletes. Training a basic level of strength can help to increase your work capacity, and improve your performance.

Diet

If you are attempting to maintain your weight and energy levels then you may need to eat slightly more when you add more exercise to your training program. As a rule of thumb, weight lifting burns 8-10 Calories per minute. For most people, a post-workout protein shake should be enough to supply their bodies with the energy and protein they need to repair their muscles and gain strength.

A high protein diet is always a good idea if you lead an active lifestyle, but the importance of healthy eating cannot be over-emphasized if you are active in sports and do extra training too. If you prefer to eat your Calories instead of drinking them in a protein shake, then think 'Chicken and vegetables' rather than 'fast food'.

'As a rule of thumb, weight lifting burns 8-10 Calories per minute.'

Summing Up

- Training for a sport is a big commitment. Make sure that you talk to your coach before adding any extra exercises to your training regimen. Your coach will be able to give you advice specific to your situation.

- Also, make sure that you get plenty of rest, and eat enough to sustain your training. If you suffer an injury, don't be shy about taking some time off. Give yourself plenty of time to recover before getting started with your sport again. The weights will still be there once you've recovered.

6

Getting More from Your Weight Training

When you first start training, the results come in pretty quickly. Whether your motivation is to train for weight loss, to get stronger, or just to feel healthier, the early stages of training offer rapid results. After you've been training a while, however, you may find that things start to slow down. At this point, it's easy to lose motivation. Don't give up! If you keep working hard, and working smart, the results will keep coming in.

Getting past the plateau

The point at which results slow down is often referred to as a plateau. Where you once saw your weight going down each week, or the amount you could lift going up, your chart of your performance starts turning into a flat line.

Plateaus are usually temporary. The important thing is to not give up. If you've been following the same program for more than a couple of months, you might need to switch things up a little bit. If you're not enjoying your workouts or feeling constantly tired and sore, then there could be something wrong with the way you're training. Ask yourself the following questions:

Are you getting enough sleep?

'You won't get very far if you follow the same program for years on end.'

Most people need eight hours sleep a night. If you're getting less than that, then it could be impacting your ability to recover from your workouts. If you're burning the candle at both ends because of work and family commitments, maybe it's time to start learning to say no to people, and start putting yourself and your health first?

When was the last time you took a break from training?

It's easy to get carried away with training – especially when you're just starting out. Results come in quickly, and the energy buzz you get from working out is hard to beat. But, even exercise can be bad if you do too much of it. In the weight training world, we call taking a break deloading. There are two ways to de-load:

- Active rest – instead of training at your usual levels, knock the weights down to 50% of your one-rep max, and do a few more reps. This way, your muscles get a chance to recover, but you still feel like you're doing something. If you hate breaking from your routine, this is a good method – it allows you to keep going to the gym, but still lets you rest.

- Inactive rest – with this method, you stop doing any weight training for a week. Instead of going to the gym you could stay at home, or go to the cinema, or do whatever you want. For some people, the mental break offered by this method is almost as useful as the physical break.

When you return to your usual routine, you should feel refreshed, and you may even find that you feel stronger.

Is it time to change your program?

You won't get very far if you follow the same program for years on end. Your body will adapt to whatever you throw at it, so to keep progressing, it's a good idea to alter your program every now and then. Just make sure that when you change to a new program, you give it a fair chance. It can take around six weeks to start seeing results. If you change your program every couple of weeks you will get nowhere.

Are you eating right?

If you're trying to lose weight, make sure that you're eating at an appropriate deficit (too low is as bad as too high). If you're trying to gain strength, make sure that you're eating enough, and that you're getting plenty of protein.

Is it time for a refeed?

Some people like to follow a 'clean' diet most of the time, and have one meal every couple of weeks where they treat themselves to something that wouldn't normally fit into their diets. As long as it's just one meal – and not a full day of junk food – this approach can work well. If you're feeling tired and bored of your diet, it's certainly worth a try.

Supplements

The supplement industry is big business, and there are a lot of scammers out there, but there are a lot of useful products too.

Supplements are designed to do exactly what their name implies – to supplement an already good diet and exercise regimen. Supplements are not going to do your work for you. If your diet is all over the place, or you don't work hard in the gym, then supplements won't help you.

Your goal should be to eat a rich and varied diet with plenty of vitamins, minerals, carbohydrates and fats. You should get everything you need from your diet, and still have time to hit the gym several times a week. Of course, very few people can actually manage that – so that's where supplements come in.

Which Supplements are Worth the Money?

If you've ever went to an exercise store or a health food store, you'll have noticed the huge racks full of supplements, diet aids, pills, and powders. If the marketing hype is to be believed, you need a supplement for every organ, every body part, and every ailment you've ever heard of! Fortunately, for most people there's just a few core supplements that are really important.

A Multi-Vitamin / Mineral

You may already be taking a multi-vitamin, but if you're not, then this is the first supplement that you should consider. It's a good way to round off your diet and make sure that you're getting all the vitamins and minerals you need.

You don't need to spend a lot of money on these. Even the low cost store's own brand ones will do. You're not looking to get all of your nutrition from one pill – just give your diet a helping hand.

A Protein Shake

Protein shakes are a good way to get more protein into your diet, and they can be a useful post-workout treat for your taste buds, and for your muscles.

Protein shakes come in many different forms and flavours. The most common types are Whey, Casein, Egg, and Soy protein.

- Whey protein is the staple of many athletes' plans; partly because it's quickly digested, and partly because it's inexpensive. Whey is a by-product of cheese production, so if you're vegan you will want to avoid it. If you're vegetarian, check what other animal products are present in the powder – most manufacturers use production processes that are suitable for vegetarians, but some do not. When you take whey, your blood amino acid levels, and protein synthesis, will peak within 40 minutes.

- Casein is a milk protein (so again, no-go for Vegans). It takes longer to digest than Whey. It takes three to four hours for your blood amino acids and protein synthesis to peak after taking Casein. The peak is lower, but this is not necessarily a bad thing.

- Egg Protein is more expensive than Whey, but it has a better amino acid profile. It also digests more quickly than Caesin (digesting within 1.5-3 hours).

- Soy is the only complete non animal protein. If you're vegan it's the logical choice. Soy protein is rich in Glutamine and flavones, and is thought to have a range of health benefits beyond just helping you build muscle. Some studies have suggested that Soy can increase your estrogen levels, but you'd have to consume a huge amount of Soy for it to have any noticeable impact.

If the above list makes it sound like all proteins are useful, well, that's because they are! For people who aren't on a special diet, egg is a good general protein, Whey is great for a post-workout shake (the quick digestion means that your body gets access to protein exactly when it needs it most), and Casein is ideal just before bed. For Vegans, Soy is a good choice as a general shake to help increase their protein intake.

You can take protein shakes with water, or with milk. Most people find they taste best served cold, and prepared using either a whisk or a shaker. Sports bottles with shakers can be purchased quite cheaply at most sports stores.

Creatine

Creatine is a popular supplement that weight lifters use in order to increase their strength, and improve the quality of their workouts.

Creatine is found naturally in meat, fish, and animal products. Most people can get at least one or two grams of creatine per day from their diet alone, but vegetarians will struggle to get enough, because there are only trace amounts of it in plants. The human body is able to synthesize its own creatine from arginine and glycine, however, so most healthy vegetarians will find their basic needs are met by that synthesis.

Athletes, however, may find that they need more creatine than the body can produce by itself, and that's why supplementation is so useful.

Creatine is taken orally. It is available in pill and powder form. The most convenient way to take creatine, in my opinion, is to mix it with your post-workout protein shake.

To Load or Not To Load?

Most creatine brands tell you to start with a 'loading phase' where you take a high dose – often up to 20g/day, for one week. At the end of this loading phase you drop down to a dose of 5g/day for a period of one month. Then you take some time off the supplement, before starting again.

'For people who aren't on a special diet, egg is a good general protein.'

The loading phase helps you to feel the beneficial effects of the creatine more quickly, but recent studies have found that there is no long term benefit to doing the loading phase. One such study, conducted by researchers at Washington State University, tested the effects of creatine on two groups – one that did the loading phase, and the other that took only the maintenance dose for the full period of the trial. At the end of the trial, both groups showed a benefit compared to the non-creatine control group, but the loading phase had no impact on long term results.

So, unless you need fast results – perhaps because you're training for a competition, there's no need to waste money taking a quadruple dose for a week!

Side effects

Some people have noticed that creatine makes them feel a little bloated. This is down to intracellular water retention. If you look for Micronized Creatine Monohydrate, you should find that any bloating you experience is minimal, but it's something to bear in mind if you are planning a trip to the beach any time soon!

The good news is that the bloating goes away almost as soon as you stop taking the supplement.

'Staying fit and healthy is a life-long proposition.'

A final word about supplements

Most dietary supplements are perfectly safe for healthy adults. However, if you have a pre-existing health condition then it's worth checking with your doctor before introducing anything new to your diet.

Also, don't try to use dietary supplements to self-medicate any health complaints. If you have any concerns about your health, speak to a trained medical professional.

Staying Motivated

Staying fit and healthy is a life-long proposition. It's easy to be motivated when you first start, and you can see the results each and every workout, but after a while things start to slow down, and working out can become a routine, or worse, a chore!

Staying motivated can be challenging, but there are a few things that you can do to make your gym session something you look forward to:

- Work out with a friend – Having someone to encourage you to go to the gym when you can't be bothered can be invaluable in more ways than one. Not only will your gym buddy make sure that you attend, they can also spot you on your lifts, and help you track your progress. Just make sure they really do want to work out, rather than just chat. A disinterested gym buddy can drag you down.

- Set smaller, more specific goals – When you first started, your goals may have been something general – such as 'lose weight', or 'get rid of my flabby arms'. Once you've achieved that goal, you need something else to motivate you. Pick something, and work on it. Your new goal could be 'shave a second off my circuit training time each workout', or 'add 2% to my lifts'. Just make sure that the goal is challenging, but measurable and achievable.

- Compete – Some people find having something specific and public to work towards hugely motivating. Depending on your strengths, you could sign up for a competition. There are competitions for all kinds of athlete. If you're proud of how you look, step on stage and show it! If you're proud of how strong you are, why not see how you compare to other people your size? Find a competition that interests you, sign up, and get training. The thought of having to demonstrate your skills in public will be a huge motivator!

Types of Competition

There are lots of competitions that are loosely related to weight training, including:

Powerlifting

Power lifting is a sport that involves the Squat, Bench Press, and Deadlift. Power lifters are divided into weight classes, and compete against people in their own weight class to see who can move the most weight in each of the above lifts.

The three lifts used in power lifting competitions are quite easy to learn, and you don't need a lot of equipment to get started. The power lifting community is a friendly and inviting one, and the philosophy is that you are not competing against the other lifters, but against your previous total. Newcomers are encouraged to test their skills and see how much they can lift, then try to beat that figure at the next competition.

Olympic Lifting

Olympic lifting is more well-known than power lifting in the mainstream. The sport involves performing the 'Snatch' and the 'Clean and Jerk'. These lifts were not described in this book because they are difficult to learn, and can be dangerous if performed incorrectly. However, you shouldn't let that put you off!

Olympic lifting is a challenging sport that requires speed, power, and co-ordination. If you want to learn how to perform the lifts, the best thing to do is join a gym that offers coaching in those lifts. The Olympic lifting community is a fairly small one compared to other sports, but competition is fierce, and there are some very skilled, and strong, lifters!

You can learn more about power lifting and Olympic lifting at: http://www.britishweightlifting.org.

Strongman/Strongwoman

'There are "events days" up and down the country where people interested in strongman training can get together to practice everything from truck pulling to working with atlas stones.'

You may have seen competitions such as the 'World's Strongest Man' on TV. There are lots of similar competitions that involve feats of strength such as the log press, atlas stones, tyre flipping, and truck pulling. These competitions are open to men and women, and they are a lot of fun!

Strongman competitions test strength, power, speed, and endurance.

You can do a lot of training for strength competitions with just basic equipment such as dumbbells and barbells, but if you plan to compete then you will need to do some training that relates directly to the events in the competition. There are 'Events days' up and down the country where people interested in strongman training can get together to practice everything from truck pulling to working with atlas stones.

You can learn more about becoming a Strongman / Strongwoman here: http://sugdenbarbell.co.uk/articles/So-You-Want-To-Be-A-Strongman

Bodybuilding and related disciplines

Women's bodybuilding is divided into several different disciplines, they are: Bodybuilding, fitness, figure, and bikini. Each discipline has a different focus.

- Bodybuilding – Bodybuilding competitions focus on muscle mass. Bodybuilding competitors are judged on their symmetry, how much muscle they have, how firm and defined they look, and their vascularity. There is a posing routine involved, but the poses are designed to show off the competitor's muscles.

- Fitness – Fitness competitors tend to look a little more feminine than bodybuilders, but they're still lean and muscular. Fitness competitors are not just judged on how they look, they're also judged on the routine that they perform. Fitness routines require a lot of skill, and often include minor elements of gymnastics.

- Figure – Figure competitors are judged on their shape and symmetry. They aren't expected to be as lean or muscular as Fitness or Bodybuilding competitors, but they are still expected to have some definition. There is some posing involved, but competitors are not expected to do a fitness routine.

- Bikini – These competitions are more pageant-like. With bikini, no one look is favoured. Competitors are expected to be in-shape, but have a look that favours their body type.

If you're planning on entering any of the above competitions, give yourself plenty of time to prepare. It can take a year or more to get ready for your first fitness show, and even longer to get into bodybuilding shape.

It's better to give yourself longer than you need to get ready than it is to step on stage un-prepared. Showing up to a fitness or bodybuilding show looking too small, or too soft, is insulting to the other competitors that have worked incredibly hard to get to where they are today.

If you're a long way off from contest shape, then one thing you could do in the short term is enter a transformation competition. There are many of these taking place on bodybuilding communities online. They're a great way to track your progress and stay motivated while working towards your long term goal of getting on the stage.

You can learn more about bodybuilding and related disciplines at:
http://www.ukbff.co.uk/about.html

Your First Competition

So, you've found a sport, and you've decided to enter a competition. Now, every sport has different rules and requirements, but there are some things that are consistent across them all.

Hopefully, the competition you've chosen is several months away, and you've got plenty of time to train. In the short term, just keep training as you normally would, but keep your eye on your goals.

A couple of weeks before the competition, you'll want to start taking it easy. Don't stop training altogether – the last thing you want is to end up feeling out of shape and out of practice – but don't start changing up your routine too much, and don't ramp up your activity level. You want to be injury free, and have plenty of energy when it comes to competition day.

If your competition has weight classes, pick a weight class that you can be close to the top of, if at all possible. If you're just a pound or two above a given weight class, you might be able to lose some weight to fit into that class on competition day. Don't try to cut more than a couple of pounds though, especially for your first competition. Cutting weight is hard work, and can leave you tired, stressed, and drained, which is never a good thing!

Try to stick to your usual routine in the days leading up to the competition. Don't eat or drink anything different. If a friend at the gym starts telling you about this amazing protein bar that gives you loads of energy, politely decline. The day before your competition is not a good time to start experimenting with new food.

Make sure you arrive early on competition day. Take a book or an MP3 player with you, and also take snacks that you know you get on with, and that won't spoil. Take plenty of liquids too. Expect to have a lot of waiting around to do, and try to stay busy so you don't get too stressed.

If you're entering a lifting competition, try to keep your energy levels up. It's important that you warm up properly, but don't over-do it and tire yourself out before it's your time on the platform. For your first lift, pick something that you know you can do. That way you have a score posted on the score boards and don't have to worry if you miss one of your later lifts.

If you're entering a bodybuilding competition then you will want to make sure that you keep your energy levels up, but don't eat or drink too much before you step on stage. Different people have different strategies for managing this, and discussing those would be beyond the scope of this book. The best thing to do is consult your coach or trainer for advice specific to your own circumstances.

Whatever you do, just remember to stay calm, and have fun. If you win, well done! If not, congratulate yourself for training hard, and having the courage to step on to the stage or the platform. By even doing that you have elevated yourself above the armchair critics and you've also gained valuable experience. Hopefully this will be the first competition of many, and you'll have a lot of success to look forward to.

'Whatever you do, just remember to stay calm, and have fun. If you win, well done! If not, congratulate yourself for training hard.'

Summing Up

- Weight training is a wonderful sport. Different people train for different reasons. Some people compete, some people supplement training for a different sport with some weight training, and others never go any further than just lifting to test their muscle versus the metal and the forces of gravity.

- Everyone is different, and no one choice is more valid than any other. The important thing is that you are doing something to improve your health and well being, and that you enjoy what you are doing.

- Stay safe, lift heavy, and have fun.

7

Injury Recovery and Prevention

Sadly, injuries are a part of life. If you're engaging in a sport, there's always the risk of a training related injury, and if you're a sedentary person with a desk job, you can still get hurt just through day to day activities. How many times have you heard of someone hurting a rib by coughing, or 'throwing their back out' picking up something small and light? Those things may sound crazy, but they can happen.

Keeping fit can reduce the risk of getting injured from day to day activities, but it brings its own challenges. If you train too much (e.g. train every day of the week and don't give your muscles time to recover), or have an accident while training, you could get injured. Fortunately, most injuries are minor, and can be treated quite easily, so as long as you don't ignore them you'll be able to get back to your training after a short time off.

Preventing injury

The old saying 'prevention is better than cure' definitely applies here. Most injuries, especially ones sustained by people new to weight training, are preventable with just a few precautions.

The most common causes of injury are:

- Bad form in exercises
- Misuse of exercise equipment
- Training without warming up
- Over training
- Ignoring warning signals and training with a minor injury

Let's go through those one by one:

Bad form in exercises

A common mistake is to watch someone doing an exercise, and just copy them – without understanding what they're doing. That's OK for some of the simpler exercises, but for more complex compound movements that involve heavy weights it's a bad idea. Unless you've had someone explain exactly where you should stand and how you should grip the bar to do a deadlift, you're risking injuring your back by trying to pick up an incredibly heavy bar the wrong way.

Even people who know how to perform an exercise sometimes let their form go. Sometimes they're having a bad day, sometimes they just do an exercise wrongly on the last rep because they're exhausted, and other times they're doing what lifters call 'ego lifting'. This is a recipe for disaster. Sure, you can move more if you employ a bit of swinging and let momentum help you – but you're not in control of the weight.

Don't fall into the trap of lifting with your ego. Stick to slow, controlled movements with weights that you find heavy, but are able to move safely, and you'll reduce your risk of injury.

Misuse of exercise equipment

Lots of things fall into this category. As you gain experience and experiment with different programs you may see people modifying exercise equipment to do some interesting new exercises with them. Personally, I wouldn't go as far as to say that exercise equipment should only ever be used for exactly what the manufacturer designed it for, but I would say that you should treat exercise equipment with respect, and engage your common sense at all times.

To me, misuse of exercise equipment means:

- Dropping dumbbells after curling (believe it or not, even hammertone plates bounce if you drop them on some surfaces)

- Bench pressing or squatting with a different amount of weight on each side of the bar.

- Unloading all the weight from one side of a barbell, leaving weight on the other side so it's precariously balanced on the rack

- Attempting heavy weight lifts without a spotter

- Attempting to do barbell squats while balancing on a bosu ball (yes, I've seen people do that).

Those are just a few examples, ranging from the 'easy to forget' to the 'just plain dangerous'. Essentially, if you remember that those plates are dense, heavy chunks of metal or rubber that could really hurt you if they landed on you, you'll act in a way that will reduce your risk of injury.

Not warming up

This goes for any sport, really. Whether you're a basketball player, gymnast, or power lifter, you can't expect to perform at your best when you're not warmed up, and it's entirely possible you'll injure yourself if you try to jump straight in to your chosen activity.

With weight training, in particular, you need to work up to your heaviest weights. There are many reasons for this – first, it gives your muscles a chance to adapt to the load, second, it allows you to perform more repetitions (even the ones that feel fairly light are still giving you some benefit), and third, it lets you prepare for the exercise and work out any problems you may have. It's much better to realise that your grip is wrong, or the spotter pins are in the wrong place, when you're moving an empty bar than to get caught out while trying to move your five rep max.

Over Training

Sometimes it's easy to get carried away with training. Either you're enjoying it so much that you don't want to stop doing it, or you're in a hurry for results and make the mistake of thinking that if some training is good, more training is always better.

Injuries are more likely if you train every single day and don't get enough rest, or if you decide to try to cram too many exercises into one day. Training too much is a waste of time anyway. Your body needs time to recover, and even competitive athletes take time off, or train on a reduced schedule every now and then. In weight training circles, this practice is called a deload – we'll discuss those later in this chapter

Not listening to warning signals

'Injuries are more likely if you train every single day and don't get enough rest.'

If you're in pain, then your body is trying to tell you something. The best thing to do is to stop as soon as you feel pain. Of course, pain isn't the same as strain. Expect to feel tired, and even a little sore, when you're exercising. You'll quickly learn to tell the difference between being sore after a good workout, and being in pain.

If you're feeling pain, stop what you're doing. If the pain keeps coming back, or takes a long time to go away, then see a doctor. Don't just assume that you were doing something wrong in a particular exercise, and that you'll be OK. The site of the pain isn't always the source, or cause of the pain – sometimes pain from one part of the body can be felt elsewhere, and sometimes bad form in an exercise can cause injury to the supporting muscles, rather than the ones you'd expect to bear the brunt of the lift.

Always consult a doctor if you feel persistent pain when exercising.

Aiding recovery – simple treatments

Minor sports injuries can be treated at home using four simple steps, which can be remembered with the acronym RICE, which stands for Rest, Ice, Compression, Elevation.

- Rest: Stop using the affected bodypart. It may be frustrating to be out of training for a couple of weeks, but think of it this way; if you train while injured, you could end up out for months instead.

- Ice: A cold compress applied to the affected area will provide short term pain relief, and also reduce swelling. If you don't have a cold compress, a bag of frozen food from your freezer will do, but wrap it in a towel first. Don't apply ice directly to your skin, and limit applications to time periods of 20 minutes or less. The last thing you want is a case of frostbite on top of your injury!

- Compression: Wrapping the affected area with a support or sports bandage can reduce swelling. This will encourage healing, and could also offer some pain relief. Take care not to wrap the bandage too tight – the goal is to reduce swelling, not prevent blood flow.

- Elevation: Elevate the affected area to prevent swelling. For example, if you've hurt your knee or ankle, lie down with your legs supported by a couple of pillows.

Heat treatment

Ice treatment is good for recent, acute injuries – for example strains, sprains, or bruises. However, if you have an over-use related injury, heat treatment can be helpful. Unlike ice treatment, where you apply the compress after the injury occurs, heat treatment is beneficial if done before the activity in question.

Applying a warm compress to the affected area relaxes and loosens the tissues, and encourages blood flow.

Most Chemists sell gel packs which are suitable for both heating and freezing, and can be re-used. These packs often come with a washable cloth cover which prevents you from getting burns or frostbite. If you don't have one of those pads, then you could use cloths soaked in warm water. Take care that whatever you use is not excessively hot.

Supplements to aid recovery

The supplement market is full of companies promoting miracle pills and herbal remedies. It can be hard to navigate all the advertisements and find the things that really do work.

There are a few supplements that have, over the years, stood the test of time and repeated clinical trial. These supplements should be safe for a healthy adult to take. However, if you have any pre-existing medical conditions, it's always wise to check with your doctor before starting to take supplements.

Glucosamine

Glucosamine is a naturally occurring amino-sugar which is used by the body to produce certain proteins, which are then used in the production of joint cartilage. Glucosamine is often recommended to sufferers of osteoarthritis, and it is also popular among athletes that experienced joint pain. Early clinical trials found that long term consumption of glucosamine was effective in terms of promoting healing and reducing pain, however more recent studies are less conclusive.

Chrondroitin Sulfate

Chondroitin Sulfate is often taken in conjunction with Glucosamine. Chondroitin Sulfate is thought to increase the effectiveness of Glucosamine. Chrondoitin Sulfate is an important part of cartilage. It helps cartilage resist compression. Supplementation of Chrondoitin Sulfate is thought to relieve joint related pain and improve functional disability. If taken in conjunction with Glucosamine, it is thought to improve the effectiveness of Glucosamine.

Omega-3 (Fish Oil)

Fish oil is one of those supplements that is supposed to cure all ills. It has been touted as having benefits for everything from cardiovascular health to recovery from traumatic brain injury. It's certainly beneficial in that it contains 'good' cholesterols, but what we're interested in here is its anti-inflammatory properties. However, Omega-3 is also an anti-coagulant – so if you're already taking medication that thins the blood, it's best to speak to your doctor before taking Omega-3.

A Multivitamin

I've included this one in the list because it's something that everyone should consider. Even if you think you have a pretty good diet, it's easy to miss out on essential nutrients. You don't need to take an expensive one. Personally, I use a stores own-brand multivitamin that also contains iron. I buy several packs when they're on special offer, so it comes to less than £1.50 a month. That's a small price to pay for the benefits.

There are many other supplements out there, but for most people they're a waste of money. If you're vegetarian you might want to consider adding protein to your list of supplements, but for most people, s balanced diet, careful exercise, and plenty of rest is all that most people need.

Before you start taking any supplements, speak to your doctor – or at the very least the pharmacist. Tell them about any medication you're taking, and any medical conditions you have. Even if someone you know is already taking a supplement, you should still check that it's safe for you. Sometimes medications and supplements (even herbal ones) can interact in surprising ways!

Deloading to prevent injury

Deloading is the concept of spending a short period of time lifting lighter weights to give your body time to recover. Most weight training programs run for a set period of time – typically six to ten weeks. During that time you'll spend a lot of time lifting heavy weights. Towards the end of the program, you may find that you're not performing as well in your workouts as you'd like. Maybe you're tiring out quickly, maybe you're failing on some sets – or maybe you're just not able to increase the amount you lift as often as you'd like.

That's usually a sign that it's time to deload. Deloading lets your muscles, and your mind, recover.

Deloading is NOT stopping lifting completely. Instead of stopping, you work out with lighter weights for a week or two. During that time you can focus on form. The workouts are less stressful to your body, but you're still sticking to a routine, and you're still getting some exercise.

When you come back from the deload you should have lots of energy, and hopefully continue to progress with your lifting.

'Deloading is the concept of spending a short period of time lifting lighter weights to give your body time to recover.'

Training while recovering from injury

The title of this section may sound strange considering I have spent the bulk of this chapter emphasizing that time off and recovery are vital. However, there's a lot to be said for staying active, as long as you do so in a safe, and responsible manner.

This doesn't mean train through pain – if an activity will aggravate your injury, don't do it.

Staying active will make your return to exercise easier once you have recovered. By sticking to your routine, and going to the gym / making time to exercise at home on your usual days, you'll keep exercise a part of your lifestyle. If you just stop training, there's always the risk that you'll get used to a more sedentary routine, and find it harder to 'get back on the horse'.

Staying active encourages your body to hold on to muscle, even in areas that you aren't currently exercising. If you're raising your heart rate then the increased circulation can be beneficial too.

Finding Suitable exercises

The first step towards remaining active is to find something that you can do. If you've injured your legs, you probably won't want to be squatting or doing deadlifts. If you've injured your right arm, then you won't be doing traditional barbell bench (or a standard squat where you're holding the bar using both hands!). However, there will be exercises that you can do.

A few likely candidates:

'If you're having difficulty sleeping, try examining your "sleep hygiene".'

- Dumbbell exercises – several were described in Chapter 2. Dumbbell exercises let you focus on the muscles you can work. Rest the injured body part, or train it with lighter weights if your doctor gave you the OK

- Bodyweight exercises – if you don't have dumbbells, or you're recovering from a serious injury and need to start gently, then bodyweight exercises give you a lot of options.

- Cardio – low intensity cardio is good for overall fitness, and exercise bikes, rowing machines, and similar devices could be good options for working out without stressing your injuries. There's no need to spend hours on the cardio machines though!

As time goes on, you'll be able to gradually re-introduce new exercises to your program. Don't be tempted to pick up where you left off, though. Start with low weight, and gradually work up to your previous levels. Patience is important here to avoid re-injury.

Also, make sure that you get plenty of rest. Not just rest as in 'time you're not training', but good quality sleep.

Sleep tips

If you're having difficulty sleeping, try examining your 'sleep hygiene':

- Avoid having caffeinated drinks in the evening
- Save the bedroom for sleep – don't work on your laptop, watch TV, etc, while in bed

- Try to follow the same routine every night – e.g. brush your teeth, comb your hair, read a book for 30 minutes, then go to bed. This 'winding down' will become routine

- Don't eat a large meal just before bed, but try not to go to bed hungry either. Perhaps a night time snack could become part of your routine?

- If you can't sleep, don't lie in bed wide awake. Get up and do something, then return to bed when you're tired.

- Getting enough sleep won't just make you have more energy for day to day activities, it will also help you to recover from injuries faster.

Help List

The following websites are useful resources for those looking to take their weight training further. The list is not exhaustive, however it should provide a good starting point for finding more specialist information.

General Resources

Bodybuilding.com

www.bodybuilding.com

Despite its name, Bodybuilding.com caters to a wide range of people. If you are interested in getting fit – whether that's to improve your performance at a sport, get healthier, or just look better on the beach, then you'll find valuable tips in the articles section, and a great support network on the forums.

Crossfit

www.crossfit.com

Crossfit is a strength and conditioning training program that covers a broad range of activities. Rather than focusing on pure strength, or aesthetics, or endurance, crossfit practitioners train to get an overall level of performance, using kettlebells, medicine balls, and other exercise equipment to get a great all-over workout.

ExRx

http://exrx.net

ExRx.net is a comprehensive exercise directory. If you would like to expand your training with exercises to target specific muscle groups, or exercises that will help with a particular sport, then this directory will help you. The site also includes information about fitness testing, injury prevention, and aerobic condition.

Livestrong.com

www.livestrong.com

Livestrong.org and the Lance Armstrong Foundation work together to help people lead a healthier life, and fight the battle against cancer. There's lots of good health and fitness advice on the Livestrong site.

Starting Strength

http://Startingstrength.com

Mark Rippetoe is an American Strength Coach that has published several books on strength training and weight lifting program design. His programs are simple and effective, and his site offers some good advice.

Diet and Nutrition

Calorie Gallery

www.calloriegallery.com

Calorie Gallery is a visual reference guide to the number of Calories in various foods. Instead of telling you how many Calories are in a specific food, it shows you a picture of a 200 Calorie portion. This makes it easy to see how Calorie dense each food is, and helps you make wiser food choices.

Calorielab

www.calorielab.com

Calorielab has some fairly comprehensive information about the nutritional breakdown of food from popular chain restaurants. The site is not UK focused, but it does include several UK restaurants, and is a valuable resource for those who wish to manage their diet without having to cut out restaurant visits.

FitDay

www.fitday.com

FitDay is a website that offers a free online diet and weight loss journal. You can use the tools on the website to track your Calorie intake and expenditure, as well as keep track of your macronutrients, and your exercise regime. If you don't like using web applications, then there is a standalone application available, although that requires a one off payment to download.

Weight Loss Resources

www.weightlossresources.co.uk

A comprehensive UK online Calories and nutrition database with Calorie, carbohydrate, protein, fat, fibre and alcohol values. An exercise database that tells you how many Calories you've burned doing a wide range of exercise activities and online food and exercise diaries to help you keep track of Calories consumed and burned throughout the day.

Powerlifting and Weightlifting

If you enjoy weight training, and would like to take your hobby one step further, then these associations will help you get started.

British Natural Bodybuilding Federation

www.bnbf.co.uk

The British Natural Bodybuilding Federation was formed in 2000, and organizes Bodybuilding, Physique, and Figure competitions for natural (drug free) competitors.

British Weight Lifting

www.britishweightlifting.org

If you'd like to learn more about the Olympic Sport of weightlifting, then the website of British Weight Lifting (originally called the British Weightlifters Association), is a good place to start. The site has information about joining the association, competitions, courses, and clubs.

Great Britain Powerlifting Federation

www.gbpf.org.uk

The Great Britain Powerlifting Federation is was formed out of the Powerlifting branch of the British Weightlifters Association. It is part of the International Powerlifting Federation and the European Powerlifting Federation, and aims to promote drug-free competition at all levels – from local competitions to national and international championships.